# PREPARE TO BE AMAZED

## BY MARY SCHENDLINGER

ANNICK PRESS

TORONTO + NEW YORK + VANCOUVER

Text © 2005 Mary Schendlinger
Line drawings © 2005 Warren Clark

**Annick Press Ltd.**

We acknowledge the support of the Canada Council for the Arts, the Ontario Arts Council, and the
Government of Canada through the Book Publishing Industry Development Program (BPIDP) for our
publishing activities.

The publisher wishes to acknowledge a publication by Alfabeta Bokförlag in Stockholm, and the book's
author, Lasse Råde, for the inspiration behind this book.

Edited by Pam Robertson
Copy-edited by Elizabeth McLean
Cover design by Irvin Cheung. Interior design by Irvin Cheung and Peter Pimentel/iCheung Design
Photo research by Mary Rose MacLachlan
Cover images courtesy the Nielsen Poster Collection and David Copperfield

**Cataloging in Publication Data**
Schendlinger, Mary, 1948–
    Prepare to be amazed : the geniuses of modern magic / written by Mary Schendlinger.

Includes bibliographical references and index.
ISBN 1-55037-927-5 (bound).—ISBN 1-55037-926-7 (pbk.)
1. Magicians—Biography—Juvenile literature.   2. Magic—History—Juvenile literature.  3. Tricks—Juvenile
literature.   I. Title.

GV1545.A2S34 2005         j793.8'092'2          C2005-901178-5

The text was typeset in Celeste, Suburban & The Sans

Printed in China

Published in the U.S.A. by:
Annick Press (U.S.) Ltd.

Distributed in Canada by:
Firefly Books Ltd.
66 Leek Crescent
Richmond Hill, ON
L4B 1H1

Distributed in the U.S.A. by:
Firefly Books (U.S.) Inc.
P.O. Box 1338
Ellicott Station
Buffalo, NY 14205

visit us at **www.annickpress.com**

For Julia

# CONTENTS

# INTRODUCTION

This book tells the story of modern magic, from the 1840s to the present day, through the lives of some of the most amazing magicians who ever picked up a wand.

The art of magic is as old as human beings. In ancient societies all over the world, magicians were people with special powers—the Druids of Europe, the Taoist priests of China, the healers of India, the astrologer–fortune tellers of Persia, the shamans of what is now North America, and many others. They appeared to understand the wonders and mysteries of animals, plants, storms, the sun and moon and stars, and other natural phenomena, as well as unseen forces such as ghosts and spirits.

About 2,000 years ago, the roles of these special people began to change and divide. Religious leaders, medicine men and women, and magic makers all had separate occupations.

The magicians, also called conjurors, became experts at creating exciting performances in which they seemed to work miracles. In China, magicians amazed huge audiences with juggling, acrobatics, storytelling, and tricks with coins and firecrackers. In Greece, magicians were expert puppeteers, ventriloquists, and jugglers who could also conjure up thunder and lightning, and make trumpets play without touching them.

Between about 500 and 1850 CE, conjurors had to practice their craft in secret. Religious leaders became very powerful, and punished those who held on to "pagan" ideas, such as the centuries-old belief that certain people could communicate with animals and forces of nature. For hundreds of years, magic shows were left to traveling show people. These men and women went all over Europe and parts of Asia performing on the street, at fairs, and in circuses for whatever donations they could get. They sang, danced, juggled, told stories, ate fire, swallowed swords, put on acts with trained dogs and bears, and did magic tricks. Some of them were brought into palaces to serve kings and queens. Others filled out their shows with dishonest activities such as picking pockets, telling bogus fortunes, and selling "medicine" that was really just brandy or flavored water. The conjuring was usually done by a man dressed as a wizard, with wild hair, a beard, and a tall, pointed hat. He performed in spooky candlelight and hid objects in his long, billowy robes and bulky stage props.

That was the look and feel of magic shows at the dawn of the modern age of magic, in the 1840s. Magic had changed a lot from the days when it was the power and privilege only of shamans and healers. Yet all magicians—even the more unsavory street magicians of the Middle Ages—had one thing in common: they had unusual ways of seeing the world around them and they could change the ways in which other people saw it, as well.

Today's magicians have that same special quality. They are experts at creating illusion—making us see with our eyes an object or movement or change that we cannot have seen. A coin disappears before our eyes, only to reappear somewhere else; a flower is set on fire and turns into a real red rose; a woman is sawn in half and put back together again. That's what everyone loves about magic. It is exhilarating and fun to see someone do the impossible. Even when we know how a trick is done, it's like watching a miracle.

All great magicians have four awesome qualities. First, they are skillful. They are aces at sleight of hand—the ability to handle objects quickly and gracefully—and at misdirection, the art of making us look where they want us to look. Second, magicians are hardworking. Most begin studying magic as young children. They practice their craft every day, dream up new variations of tricks, train assistants, perform with great energy and enthusiasm, and promote their shows. Third, magicians are performers. They create just the right combination of costumes, lights, and stage sets. They roll out their tricks in the perfect order and with the perfect timing to build suspense for maximum thrills and chills. They startle the audience and charm them at the same time. And they think fast to save a trick when it doesn't go exactly as planned. Fourth, and most important, magicians believe in magic. When they perform illusions, they aren't trying to fool us—they are inviting us to go with them to a magic place.

These qualities have not changed in thousands of years, and neither have the basic conjuring tricks themselves. "All illusions are derived from five basic ideas," say Siegfried and Roy, two of the magicians featured in this book. "Appearance, disappearance, transformation, levitation, and sawing." When the ancient Egyptian conjuror Dedi of Dedsnefru performed for the great pyramid builders, he cut off the head of a pelican and magically restored it. More than 3,000 years later, the modern-day magician David Copperfield cut himself in half with an ultra high-tech laser beam and then put himself back together.

But the ways in which a conjuror can do the tricks are infinite, and it is the special style of a magician that sets him or her apart from the others. Even the approach to patter—the chatting and joking that magicians do while they are performing—varies among the great magicians. One might chatter all through his show, commenting on his own act and making outrageous puns. Another might perform in complete silence. The great Harry Houdini created an air of suspense by glaring fiercely at his spectators and challenging them to stump him.

The story of modern conjuring starts in the golden age of magic, from the 1840s to the 1950s. In the mid 1800s Jean Eugene Robert-Houdin performed on a simple stage wearing a tailored evening suit and a tidy haircut. It was the beginning of the end of the wizard-style street magician. The image of magic and magicians had been transformed.

In the 1880s, when transportation by steamship and rail suddenly got a lot easier and faster, traveling variety shows called vaudeville became wildly popular in Europe and North America.

These were live theater performances featuring music, dancing, acrobatics, comedy, and magic. Hundreds of magicians worked in these productions and a few great ones got their start in vaudeville. Among them were Adelaide Herrmann, whose opulent shows were as grand as operas; Chung Ling Soo, an American who led a double life as a dazzling Chinese conjuror; the Great Lafayette, a flamboyant quick-change artist; and Harry Houdini, a master of escape and the most famous magician of all time.

Meanwhile, the magnificent conjuror P.C. Sorcar was reviving the ancient traditions of his native India, while Harry Blackstone perfected the art of "small magic"—simple tricks that can be done by hand, with everyday objects. By 1965, when Blackstone died, vaudeville had died too, along with many other live theater shows. People in North America and Europe were going to movies or staying home to watch television, and the golden age of magic was over.

But a new age of magic was already in the works. In the 1970s, a young, skinny guy in shaggy hair and a tie-dyed T-shirt bounced onstage and then onto TV, thrilling millions of people with fun new versions of classic tricks. He was Doug Henning, and he almost single-handedly brought live magic back. Many more magicians found work, and new venues opened up to conjurors of all kinds. One of those venues was the Mirage Hotel in Las Vegas, where two young Germans named Siegfried and Roy mounted a spectacular show combining thoroughly modern special-effects technology with the most ancient form of magic: natural magic. They showed the world that big magic performances are a thing of the present, as well as the past. For David Copperfield, currently the most successful magician in the world, the sky is the limit. He works with cutting-edge technology such as lasers and satellites in creating powerful new stage illusions. Yet he too is a master at sleight of hand and will still go into the audience during his show to make an egg appear in a woman's purse.

The magicians of the modern age have been men and women, young and old, good-looking and weird-looking, shy and flamboyant. They have known glamour and excitement, as well as hardship and disaster. All of them have been skilled and determined, and all of them have had the power to amaze. Their adventures are the story of magic.

🕸🕸

You may become part of that story, too. You'll find some great tricks you can learn after each magician's tale. Have fun—and remember that, like the great magicians, you'll need to practice over and over to get it just right. Eventually, your manner will be confident, your movements will be smooth enough to deceive the eye—and people will be amazed!

THÉATRE
ROBERT-HOUDIN
8 Boul^d des Italiens
TOUS LES SOIRS
GRAND SUCCÉS
LE DÉCAPITÉ RÉCALCITRANT
Bouffonnerie Spirite
AFFICHES AMÉRICAINES CH. LEVY 10 Rue Martel PARIS

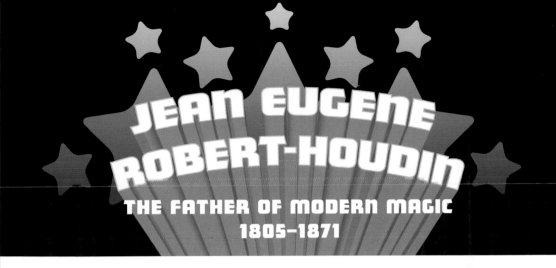

# JEAN EUGENE ROBERT-HOUDIN

## THE FATHER OF MODERN MAGIC
### 1805–1871

JEAN EUGENE ROBERT-HOUDIN (pronounced Ro-BARE Oo-DAN) is called the Father of Modern Magic because he made the art of magic respectable. In 1845 he became the first magician to appear on an uncluttered, well-lit stage, and to wear a suit and tie, rather than the sorcerer getups of the street magicians of the time. His goal was to amaze people with his skill, not a spooky atmosphere.

Robert-Houdin was a French clockmaker who invented mechanical devices in his spare time. One day when he was 20 years old, he ordered a book on clocks and the bookstore sent him a book on magic tricks by mistake. He opened the book and began reading, and he was hooked.

Soon he began to build and repair magic equipment for traveling conjurors, and he learned every sleight of hand trick he could find. Finally, in 1845, he opened his own show, and it was a hit. Not only was he refined and elegant, he performed with the magnificent automata (robots) that he had been creating for 20 years—life-sized birds that fluttered and sang, and mechanical people no taller than a cereal box that played chess, walked tightropes, and baked tiny pastries. His "Fantastic Orange Tree" burst into bloom, then produced real oranges. In those days before electric power or batteries, all of his machines worked like clocks—with gears, springs, and levers.

But it was a thrilling new act called "Second Sight" that brought Robert-Houdin real success about a year later. His 14-year-old son, Emile, would sit onstage, blindfolded. As Robert-Houdin held up personal possessions offered by people in the audience, Emile would identify them, apparently by reading his father's mind. The secret of the trick was in the spoken clues. If Robert-Houdin asked Emile, "What is this?" the item was made of gold. If he said, "Now please say what this is," it was a key. "Come now, what is this?" indicated a coin, and so on.

At first people offered things like fans, watches, umbrellas, and pocket change. Then, as stories of Emile's mind-reading feats spread through Paris, people brought more and more unusual items—books written in Greek, specialized tools, Oriental coins carved with obscure slogans. Emile could name everything, because Robert-Houdin had devised a new method of communication: the electric telegraph. This device, invented before the radio and the telephone, sent coded electric signals through a wire to spell out words. It had just become available,

but most people didn't know about it yet. It was perfect for Robert-Houdin, lover of gadgets and gizmos. He and Emile learned Morse code, and as Robert-Houdin held up each item to be identified, an assistant offstage would transmit the information to Emile through a floor plate under his feet.

Everyone in Paris knew about the marvels of Second Sight— including King Louis Philippe, who invited Robert-Houdin to put on a special show for the royal family and their guests. What an honor! Robert-Houdin dreamed up an extra-spectacular mind-reading trick and spent six days getting everything ready.

When the curtain went up in the king's theater, Robert-Houdin performed some vanishing tricks, delighted the audience with his automata, and amazed them with Emile and the famous Second Sight trick. Then he borrowed six handkerchiefs from the guests, laid them on a table near the back curtain, and covered them with a large bell. He handed small blank cards to several guests and got them to write down places where he could magically hide the hankies. Then he had the king select three of these cards and choose one hiding place. The king did so, deciding that the bundle should be buried outside, under an orange tree in the garden.

As Robert-Houdin lifted the bell to show that the handkerchiefs were still on the table, two palace servants rushed outside to guard the orange tree, making sure no one could sneak the hankies under the tree. Onstage, Robert-Houdin covered the handkerchiefs with the bell once more, waited a moment, then lifted the bell. Out flew a dove. "The handkerchiefs are gone," Robert-Houdin cried. "Behold!" In the garden, one of the guards dug around under the orange tree and unearthed a small, rusty metal box. This was taken to King Louis Philippe, and voilà!—the hankies were inside.

How did Robert-Houdin do it? When he first covered the hankies with the bell, Emile, who was behind the back curtain, reached through a trap door in the table, pulled them out, and replaced them with similar-looking handkerchiefs. He then secretly popped them into the metal box and buried the box under the tree while the guests were busy thinking up hiding places. Earlier that day Robert-Houdin had prepared some hiding-place cards of his own, which he presented to the king as though they were three of the audience's cards. Robert-Houdin knew that the king would choose the orange tree because one of the other choices was too easy and the other was too far away.

Jean Eugene Robert-Houdin performed onstage for only 10 years, and he did not invent any brand-new tricks. Yet he changed the art of magic forever—from a mysterious and slightly creepy show, to a thrills-and-chills performance that relied on skill, personality, and an amazing way with gadgets and gizmos.

# HUNCH CARD

Amaze your audience with your powers of "Second Sight"—name the card that is on the table, without seeing it or touching it.

**MATERIALS:** Two decks of playing cards with different patterns on the back; 1 envelope large enough to fit a card.

Have a friend shuffle one deck of cards, then start throwing them down on the table quickly, face down, one on top of the other. Tell your friend to stop at any point, anywhere in the deck. When she stops, pull an envelope out of your pocket and hold it up. Without opening it, say: "Okay, you shuffled the deck and you stopped where you wanted—I didn't touch the cards. But I had a hunch you would stop at that card." Lay the envelope on top of the pile. Have your friend turn up the last card that was laid down. Now have her open the envelope and take a look at your hunch card. Voilà! It is the same card.

## HOW IT'S DONE

Before the show, take any card out of the extra deck and put it in the envelope. Take the same card out of the playing deck. Lay that card on the envelope face up and put the envelope and card in your jacket or shirt pocket, with the card facing in toward your body. Put away the extra deck.

When you are before your audience, and you pull out the envelope, hold the loose card against it in such a way that the envelope and card come out together but your friend can't see the card. Lay the envelope down on the pile with the card down, so that the card ends up on top of the other cards as though it were the last card your friend dropped on the pile. The cards should be untidy so that the extra card looks natural. That's why you ask your friend to throw down the cards fast. If the stack is too neat, mess it up a bit as you lay down the envelope.

15

# ADELAIDE HERRMANN

## QUEEN OF MAGIC
## 1853–1932

**A**DELAIDE HERRMANN was a magician who always believed that more was better. She put on big, classy magic shows with extravagant sets, costumes, and decorations, and produced incredible numbers of objects out of thin air. As the first woman to run her own magic show, she also blazed the trail for other women conjurors.

Herrmann was a young, beautiful, slightly outrageous American dancer when she married Alexander Herrmann, a world-famous German magician, in 1874. At a time when women covered their bodies at all times, wearing long skirts even to ride a bicycle, Herrmann danced freely, kicking up her heels and showing her legs. Alexander had never worked with assistants, but when he put Herrmann in his show, she was a huge hit. In one of their routines, he brought out an empty picture frame, attached a sheet

17

of paper to it, drew a picture of a cocoon, and poof! The cocoon burst open and out flew Herrmann, dressed as a moth and flitting about the stage in an enchanting dance.

The Herrmanns made pots of money, but they spent it faster than they made it. When Alexander died in 1896, he left Herrmann almost penniless. In those days it was taboo for a woman to run a business, especially a theatrical business. But conjuring and dancing were the only work Herrmann knew and loved, and all she had were bookings for shows that Alexander had lined up. She put together a magic show of her own, called herself "Madame Herrmann," and went back to work.

Herrmann's shows were larger than life. She hung her stage with layers and layers of luxurious velvet drapes and plenty of fringe. She and her assistants wore sumptuous outfits decorated with beads, flowers, ruffles, and spangles. Onstage she didn't just conjure up silk, she conjured up a hundred colors of silk scarves as big as bed sheets. She didn't just produce paper streamers, she pulled a mountain of them out of a coconut shell, then lifted live ducks from the middle of the pile.

Best of all, Herrmann told stories with her magic tricks. In her "Noah's Ark" story, a big ark-shaped box with lots of cupboards in it was brought onstage. Herrmann opened all of the cupboard doors quickly, two or three at a time, to show that the ark was empty. Then her assistants filled it with water and the ark embarked on its voyage, moving about the stage with a great sloshing sound. Herrmann opened a tiny cupboard door and two doves flew out. She opened another slightly larger door and a pair of quacking ducks tumbled out and waddled off. From other doors came chickens, geese, roosters, and turkeys. Then came cats, dogs, and finally a pair each of lions and tigers (actually dogs fitted with costumes). The stage was teeming with more creatures than could possibly fit in the ark, or so it seemed. And still there was more to come. Herrmann threw open the whole side of the ark. Not one drop of water was left in it, and a young woman reclined inside. The secret of the ark illusion was to move the creatures around between the many compartments lightning fast, and to rig it up so that the water drained out through a secret tube as quickly as it was poured in.

One of Herrmann's favorite stories was the "Haunted Artist." She came onstage dressed as an artist and began to paint a picture of a woman. The artist sat down in an armchair to rest, and as she dozed, a devil burst out of the fireplace and into the room. The woman in the painting came to life and the artist awoke and danced with her. When the devil tried to steal the woman away, she leapt into the frame and turned back into a painting of herself.

Herrmann had lots of other stories. The "Temple of Magic," the "Flight of the Favorite," "A Night in Japan," "Cleopatra the Egyptian Sorceress," and the "Palace of Illusions" were just a few of many, and each show was more spectacular than the last. But they were expensive, and Herrmann was on a tight budget when she started out solo. On at least one occasion she was caught sneaking reams of silk fabric from Mexico into the United States, trying to avoid paying duty on them.

With her extravagant show, Herrmann's act was a headliner in vaudeville shows all across North America and in Europe. She was a great success in London, Paris, and every major city in America, where she was known as the Queen of Magic.

Adelaide Herrmann was still performing a few shows a week at age 73 when she finally retired. At a time when women were not even allowed to vote, she had danced and performed magic for 50 years, 30 of those with her own show. She had also brought the fun and flash of show business to the art of magic.

# CORNUCOPIA IN A PAPER BAG

Adelaide Herrmann loved to conjure up colorful flowers, silks, and feathers and fill her stage with them. You can produce lots of beautiful material, Adelaide-style, from an empty paper bag.

**MATERIALS:** Paper bag 7–8 inches (18–20 cm) wide; scarves, silk flowers, flags, hankies, and/or bits of lightweight material.

SLIT

OPENING OF "POCKET"

Show the audience the bag inside and out so they can see it is just an empty paper bag. Then hold it in front of you, reach in with your hand, and pull lots of wonderful things out of the "empty" bag.

### HOW IT'S DONE

Before the show, prepare the bag by cutting a horizontal slit in the back, 4–5 inches (10–12.5 cm) long (long enough to put your hand through) and 3 inches (7.5 cm) from the bottom. Use a very thin blade, so that the audience can't see the slit when you show them the bag.

Pin a soft plastic bag to the inside of an unbuttoned vest, shirt, or jacket, with the opening of the bag close to the open edge of the vest. It should nestle in the vest like a pocket or pouch that can't be seen from the outside. Stuff the various items into the "pocket." Leave the vest unbuttoned.

When you are before your audience, rest the paper bag on the open palm of one hand, right in front of your vest. Reach into the bag with the other hand, slip your fingers through the slit and into your "pocket," and pull the colorful pieces up through the slit and out the top of the bag.

**A** HUNDRED YEARS AGO, CHUNG LING SOO was the most famous Chinese magician in the world. Yet he was no more Chinese than the Queen of England. His real name was Billy Robinson and he was born and raised in New York City.

Robinson was eight years old when he saw his first conjuring show and fell in love with the art of magic. He read every book he could find on the subject, went to work for accomplished magicians, and spent all of his spare time practicing, until he was an expert with coins, cards, rings, doves, and more. But there were lots of good magicians around, and Robinson had trouble finding steady work.

Meanwhile, people were pouring into theaters all over North America to see the hottest new magic sensation: conjuring acts all the way from China. So Robinson took a chance. In the spring

of 1900 he applied for a show at a theater in London, England, as Chung Ling Soo, the Marvelous Chinese Conjuror. The theater said yes, and Robinson began to transform himself into Chung.

Dot, Robinson's wife and stage assistant, renamed herself Suee Seen. She and Robinson packed up their gear and moved to England. There they rebuilt and repainted everything to look Asian and bought luxurious Oriental stage outfits. Chung Ling Soo played to a sold-out theater on opening night and for many nights after that.

As Chung Ling Soo, he spat flames and fireworks from his mouth. He conjured up live wiggly goldfish and seemingly endless streams of bright-colored silk ribbon. He rubbed grains of rice between two plates until they were transformed into live birds, and he magically produced a huge knee-high bowl of water from nowhere. He moved quickly from trick to trick without saying a word.

But he was best known for the grand finale of his show—the "Bullet Catch," a terrifying trick in which rifles were fired straight at him and he appeared to save his own life by catching the bullets in midair. He set up the trick onstage as a lurid drama in which he faced a firing squad. While he took his place and was blindfolded, gunpowder and real bullets were pushed into the rifles with ramrods. Then Chung held a china plate to his chest and the gunmen aimed their weapons at his heart. The rifles were fired, Chung swept the plate through the air, the audience screamed— and, as the smoke cleared, Chung could be seen holding out the plate with the bullets on it.

Some magicians did the Bullet Catch by secretly removing the bullets when the guns were loaded, but not Chung. He rigged up special rifles with two barrels, one for the bullet and the other for a "blank" (bullet-free) charge of gunpowder and wadding. The firing pin on the gun ignited the blank charges, making a grand explosion but shooting no bullets. Chung faced the gunmen with bullets concealed in his hand. When the rifles went off, he slipped the bullets onto the plate before swinging it out for everyone to see.

Chung and Suee played their roles offstage as well as on. They lived in an apartment decorated in the Oriental style, they went everywhere dressed and made up as a Chinese couple, and they pretended that they couldn't speak English. When a real Chinese conjuror came to town and opened his act in a theater a block away from Chung's show, people went to check it out, but they came back to Chung Ling Soo.

The Birth of the Butterfly

On Saturday, March 23, 1918, Chung performed his last show. He did some warm-up tricks, then set up for the Bullet Catch. Two volunteers from the audience, British soldiers home on leave from World War I, confirmed that the bullets were real and loaded the rifles. The gunmen aimed, Chung held up his plate, the weapons exploded—and Chung crumpled and fell to the stage, real blood seeping out of a real gunshot wound. One of the rifles had rusted inside, and on that evening some gunpowder had sifted into the barrel with the bullet. When the charge was lit, both barrels fired.

Someone tore down a stage curtain and Chung was wrapped in it. He was rushed to hospital, but he could not be saved. He died at dawn the next day. That weekend the Sunday papers revealed the exciting secret that Chung Ling Soo had really been an American named Billy Robinson. But it wasn't a scandal—everyone just admired him even more for pulling off another wonderful trick.

# UPSTANDING EGG

In his "Bullet Catch" trick, Chung Ling Soo seemed to be defying the laws of nature by catching speeding bullets. You can appear to defy nature with this quick trick.

**MATERIALS:** One egg; 1/2 teaspoon (2 mL) granulated sugar; white handkerchief or other white cloth, 4 inches (10 cm) square or larger.

Challenge a friend to make an egg stand on end. Your friend can't do it, but you can.

### HOW IT'S DONE

Before the show, conceal the sugar in one hand. Place the white cloth on the table. Then ask your friend to stand the egg up on one end. After your friend tries and fails to get the egg to stand on end, reach out with both hands to pick up the egg, as though you need to handle it with special care. Just before you cup your hands around the egg, let the sugar drop from your hand into a little pile on the cloth, in such a

way that your friend won't notice it being placed there. Hold the egg for a few moments and appear to concentrate. Say some magic words, or even talk to the egg. Then hold the egg upright (wider end down) and push it gently into the pile of sugar.

Ta-da! Let the miracle sink in, then, in a single motion, pick up the gravity-defying egg and brush away the sugar.

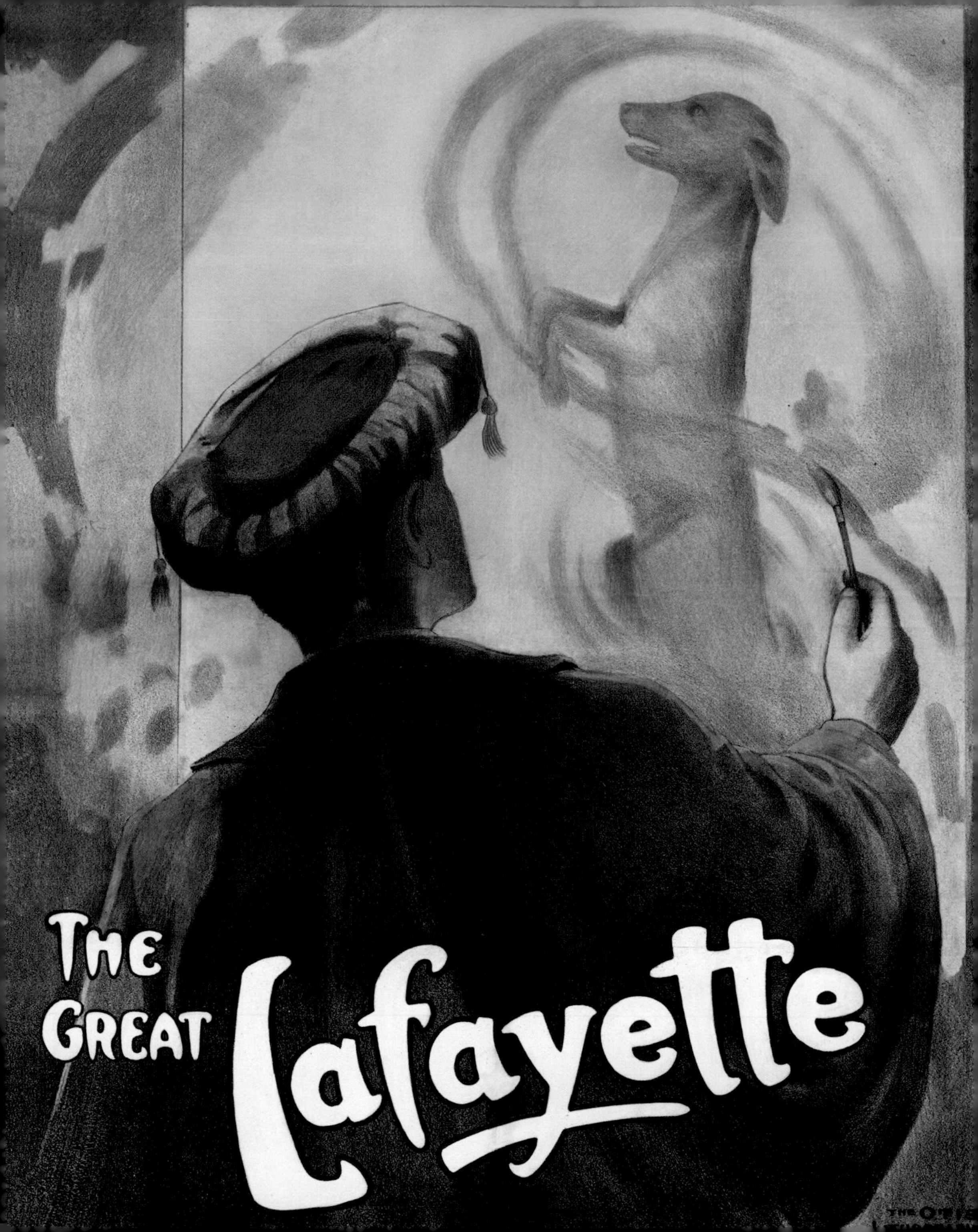
THE GREAT
Lafayette

# THE GREAT LAFAYETTE

## QUICK-CHANGE ARTIST
## 1871–1911

FOR SIGMUND NEUBERGER, life was one big costume party. He always had a lot more fun and a lot more success when he was in disguise than when he was himself.

Neuberger was 19 years old when he went to work in vaudeville shows as a quick-change artist, changing costumes and locations so quickly that he seemed to be in two places at once. He was also a terrific impersonator, and his imitation of the popular Chinese conjurors of the day made him famous overnight. He came onstage in billowy silk robes, waved a spangly cloth, and pulled a big bowl of water from it. Then he produced a flock of pigeons, a dog, a turkey, and even two little kids wearing nothing but diapers.

Show business was Neuberger's life, and now it was his living as well. In 1900 he changed his name to the more glamorous

"Lafayette," left his native Germany, and opened his own show in London, England. There, every night at the packed Hippodrome Theatre, he put on his act, which had more colors, lights, and magnificent costumes and props every week. As the curtain rose on his "Carnival of Conjuring," Lafayette dashed onstage to zippy live music that made everyone's heart beat faster, dressed in a satin costume that seemed to glow under the lights. Then he snatched live birds out of thin air and conjured up his pet dog from a shiny gold picture frame on an easel. In the blink of an eye he became a sculptor, shaping blobs of clay into the form of a woman, which magically became a real woman as fountains of water erupted all around, lit by colored lights.

In another of Lafayette's crowd-pleasing acts, he played the evil Dr. Kremser, who set out to do a horrifying experimental operation on Lafayette's pet dog, Beauty. Fortunately the dog was spared, but Kremser got his head cut off (it was magically restored later). In another story, Lafayette played an artist. His assistant stood in a fancy picture frame and Lafayette dressed him in a series of wigs, makeup, fake beards, and clothing to make him look like famous people. One of them, the czar of Russia, stepped out of the frame as Lafayette walked offstage. The czar removed his beard and wig to reveal—Lafayette! He then rushed to a basket at the side of the stage, flipped it open, and out popped the assistant.

Like any good showman, the Great Lafayette always saved the best for last—the "Lion's Bride" act. A beautiful princess survived a shipwreck, only to be captured by a powerful king. He gave her the choice of marrying him or being thrown into the cage of a huge snarling lion. She chose the lion, but in the nick of time her soldier sweetheart—Lafayette— charged in astride a huge black horse, defeated a burly guard in a thrilling sword fight, then disguised himself as the princess and took her place. Guards rushed onstage and threw him into the lion's cage. The lion roared and reared up on its back legs, then tore off its own false head to reveal—none other than Lafayette himself!

Lafayette moved so quickly that he always seemed to be in two or three places at once. How did he do it? Mostly with hidden compartments under the stage and a crowd of assistants, who looked and dressed like Lafayette. He would move around swiftly, changing places with them and darting behind bits of scenery to make his fast changes.

In real life, as himself, Lafayette wasn't nearly as much fun. At the height of his success he had 45 people working for him, and he ordered them around during rehearsals and shows as though he were a general in the army. He even expected his employees to salute him when they saw him—offstage as well as on. Lafayette reserved his tender and loving side for his dog, a gift from Harry Houdini. Beauty had a dog-sized apartment with miniature furniture, and luxuries like velvet cushions and a diamond-studded collar.

In May 1911, as Lafayette and his crew were performing at a theater in Edinburgh, Scotland, a fire started onstage. Miraculously the 3,000 spectators got out unharmed—once they realized the fire was not part of the show. But the stage area was a furnace of flame and smoke. None of the performers could escape, because Lafayette had blocked off most of the backstage exits to make sure no one sneaked in and discovered the secrets of his illusions. Nine bodies, including one assumed to be Lafayette's, were found in the stage area after the fire was put out.

It wasn't until the next morning that the last quick-change magic act of the Great Lafayette was discovered. One more body was found in a compartment beneath the stage, and the jewellery on the fingers showed this to be the real Lafayette.

Thousands and thousands of Edinburgh fans lined the streets when Lafayette's funeral procession rolled by a few days later. As it happened, Beauty had died just days before the fire, so Lafayette was buried under an elm tree with his one true love.

# DOUBLE YOUR MONEY

Magically change one dime into two dimes, almost as fast as Lafayette changed from a princess into a lion.

**MATERIALS:** Two identical pieces of paper 4 inches (10 cm) square; two dimes; glue; clear tape.

Borrow a dime from a friend and wrap it up in a piece of paper. Then talk about how great it would be to double your money whenever you want just by folding it into bits of paper, and show that the dime has changed into two dimes.

## HOW IT'S DONE

Ahead of time, stick the two papers together in the center with a blob of glue. Fold the two dimes in one paper and fasten it closed with a tiny piece of clear tape.

In front of your audience, hold the paper in your hand so that the open piece faces up and can be seen, but the folded one underneath is hidden. When you get your friend's dime, wrap it in the open piece of paper. Then turn the whole thing over in your hand while you chat on about how money multiplies when it gets wrapped up like this. While your friend is watching, quickly unfold the two dimes and take them out, making sure you don't draw attention to the tiny piece of tape. Casually scrunch up the piece of paper—with your friend's dime—and toss it on the table.

**H**ARRY HOUDINI'S SPECIALTY WAS DARING ESCAPES—from trunks, bags, handcuffs, jails, and crates thrown into the water. With his skill, his magnetic personality, and his awesome talent for advertising and publicity, he became the most famous magician who ever lived.

Houdini was born in Hungary and grew up in Wisconsin, USA. He was nine years old when he saw a magic show for the first time in 1883, and he was even more fascinated by the audience than by the illusions. As the magician cut a man into pieces, promising to restore him later, Houdini saw that people were literally on the edge of their seats, and realized that magic is most thrilling with a big dose of suspense.

Houdini hung around circuses to learn sleight-of-hand tricks with coins and cards, simple rope-tie escapes, and the crowd-

pleasing trick of swallowing a couple of packets of needles and then pulling them back out, all threaded on a long string. He worked hard to keep himself physically fit. He ran, he swam, he lifted weights, and he didn't drink or smoke. He taught himself how to hold his breath underwater for two minutes—longer than most professional swimmers.

His real name was Erich Weiss, but when he was 17 years old he renamed himself Houdini, after his hero, Jean Eugene Robert-Houdin. Then he went off to perform in circuses, variety shows, beer halls—for whoever would hire him. His favorite acts were rope-tie and handcuff escapes, which also became his hobby. He studied everything he could find about locks, keys, and manacles, he worked for a locksmith, and he practiced obsessively. He even taught the family dog how to do a simple rope-tie escape.

Houdini made the escapes more exciting for himself and his audience by daring people to tie or lock him up so that he couldn't get away. He traveled throughout North America, slipping out of handcuffs, straps, leg irons, and straitjackets. When he arrived in a town where he was going to give a show, he challenged the local police chief to lock him up, and he always broke free. The timing of these stunts could not have been better. He performed them through the 1890s, the years of the rough-and-tumble Wild West of America, when stories of outlaws and daring jailbreaks filled the newspapers.

How did Houdini do his escapes? His main tool was his physical fitness and strength. If your muscles are well developed and you puff them out when someone is tying you up, the rope will loosen a lot when you relax. Another secret was to conceal tiny keys and picks in the enclosures that he was locked into, or even in his thick, wiry hair and the callused skin on his feet.

Houdini burned with energy and strong feelings. He slept only five hours a night and spent the rest of his time arranging shows, putting up posters, talking to news reporters, practicing his magic, and thinking up new illusions. He loved his audiences and was known to spend a long time talking patiently with even the most cuckoo fans.

But if Houdini didn't like you, look out. He never forgot an insult, even a small one. If he thought a magician was a fraud, he humiliated the person in public. If he thought someone was copying his tricks, he launched a lawsuit. He gladly shared his sleight-of-hand secrets with other magicians, as they shared theirs, but not the escapes. He figured they were his and his alone. When he found out that Harry Blackstone was doing underwater packing crate escapes, he was furious. He even tried to get Blackstone thrown out of the Society of American Magicians.

Houdini never stopped dreaming up new escapes—the more heart-stopping, the better. One of them was the "Chinese Water Torture Cell," which was neither Chinese nor torture, but it sure sounded scary. Houdini showed the audience the empty cell, or tank, a plain box with a glass front. Then water was poured into the tank, and with great fanfare, he was handcuffed and lowered head first into it. Curtains were closed over the cell. A giant stopwatch ticked away onstage, while Houdini's assistants hovered anxiously. One minute... one and a half minutes... and just as you were about to start gasping for breath, Houdini stepped out, dripping wet, to take his bows.

Houdini's outdoor tricks were even more dangerous. Tens of thousands of spectators flocked to riverbanks to watch his famous bridge jumps, when he would leap into the water shackled to the max or tied up in a straitjacket, and magically reappear a few minutes later. If there was no river, he did the escape at the end of a long rope, dangling from a tall building—preferably the local newspaper offices so that everyone in town would know about it.

Houdini was so proud of his strong, hard abdomen that he often invited young men to punch him in the belly. On a beautiful October afternoon in 1926, a university student threw a punch before Houdini was ready for it. Houdini was already suffering stomach pain—possibly from appendicitis—and the blow made it worse. He struggled through a few more shows but finally collapsed. By the time he saw a doctor his appendix had become infected and he could not be saved. Harry Houdini, the world's most famous magician, died on Halloween.

# GOOFY ROPE-TIE ESCAPE

Spice up a classic Houdini routine with a little humor—get out of an impossible situation and make 'em laugh at the same time.

**MATERIALS:** two pieces of rope, each about 3 feet (just under a meter) long; bath towel (or other cloth about that size).

To prove that the rope is genuine, allow your audience to inspect it. Choose a volunteer to help you, and have her tie your wrists with the rope, then lay the towel over your bound wrists. Then have her tie your ankles. As she does so, lift the towel so that the audience, but not the volunteer, can see your hands — which are free of ties (1). Wave to the audience, then replace your hands in the ties and invite the volunteer to check that the ties are still tight.

When she goes back to work on your ankles, pull out both hands. Hold up the towel a bit with one hand, so that the audience can see your hands but the volunteer cannot. With the other hand, point at her and make exaggerated laughing motions with your face.

By now the audience will be laughing too, and the volunteer will wonder why. When she has finished tying you up, throw off the ropes and have everyone give her a big hand.

## HOW IT'S DONE

Hold your wrists together as in (2-left), with your palms cupped, and have the volunteer tie them with one square knot. Make sure you don't let her tie the knot too tight, or too far down your wrists. To get your right hand out of the tie, rotate your right hand clockwise under your left (2 right). To get back into the tie, reverse the procedure.

(1)

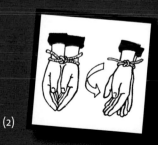

(2)

39

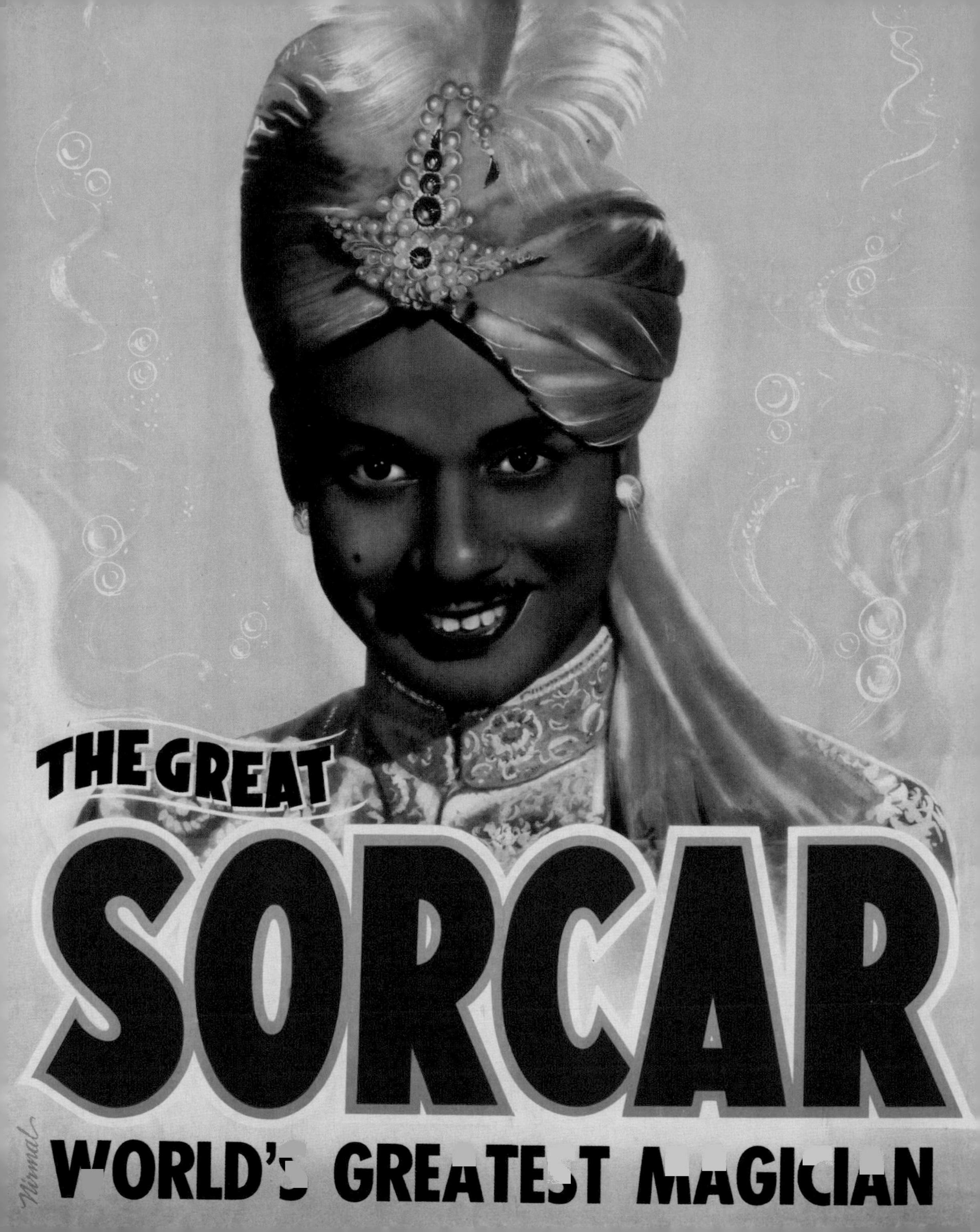
THE GREAT
SORCAR
WORLD'S GREATEST MAGICIAN
Nirmal

**P**ROTUL CHANDRA SORCAR combined the best magic tricks and traditions of India and the West (Europe and North America) to breathe new life into Indian conjuring. His skill as an artist, his astute business sense, and his knack for promoting the show made him one of the best-known magicians in the world, and he was acclaimed as the world's greatest magician by many critics, historians, and magicians of his time.

Sorcar grew up in India in the 1920s, when magic, which had been a lively and popular art for centuries, had all but died out. Conjuring was left to the *jaduwallah*—street magicians who juggled, charmed snakes, and made small objects disappear for whatever coins people would toss to them.

But Sorcar wanted to make magic—not on a dusty roadside but in a theater, and not just in India but everywhere. He had

learned the methods of his father, grandfather, and great-grandfather, who all did magic as a hobby. He practiced his craft through high school and university, and then he turned to magic full-time.

Sorcar was 21 years old when he put together his own act and traveled alone to Burma, Thailand, Singapore, and China, where he drew large audiences. He fired a gun in the air and four ducks popped out of it. He made pigeons vanish and reappear. Then came his mesmerizing "X-Ray Eyes" act. Blindfolded with blobs of plaster and a thick scarf, he invited people from the audience to come up on stage and write anything on a blackboard, in any language. Whatever they wrote, he read it aloud or duplicated it on the board. In another act, he disappeared from the stage and instantly popped up at the back of the theater, laughing and calling, "I am here!"

Like most conjurors, Sorcar exchanged tips and techniques with any magician who would talk to him. Not all of them would. Sorcar dressed like them and conjured in the Western style, but some magicians and theater owners would not cooperate with him because he was Indian. Sorcar did not give up. He just kept working hard and getting better.

As he traveled, studied, and performed, Sorcar began to understand that some Western-style tricks had been adapted from Indian magic that was centuries old. By now he had the confidence to bring these acts into his show with their Indian flavor restored. He named the show Ind-Dra-Jal (Bengali for "magic"). His orchestra played Indian-style music with bells, flutes, and drums, and incense was burned during the show. Sorcar wore silk robes, a jeweled turban with a plume, and gold slippers with long, turned-up toes.

For his "Water of India" illusion, 12 assistants lined up, each holding a large empty glass. Sorcar produced a tiny pitcher of water and filled every assistant's glass to the top, without ever refilling the itty bitty pitcher. When the assistants left the stage, they all poured the water from their glasses back into the pitcher, which magically did not overflow. For Sorcar's "Festival in Calcutta," one assistant after another wheeled an empty rack or cart onstage, and Sorcar filled every one of them with silk flowers, clocks, colorful streamers, birds, people, and even a live elephant—all conjured up out of thin air. The show got so elaborate that Sorcar and his staff needed 40 hours to set it up and rehearse. He insisted on perfection, and personally managed every detail of the production and the business from his five-story office and shop in Calcutta.

In promotion and publicity, as on stage, Sorcar didn't miss a trick. He and his staff produced a constant stream of posters, press releases, and copies of reviews, and Sorcar himself grew famous for his "X-Ray Eyes" publicity stunt: he rode a bicycle through the busiest streets of huge cities,

including Paris and New York, while wearing a heavy blindfold.

But the incident that made him famous—literally overnight—was a television performance of his hair-raising "Sawing a Lady in Half" trick. On April 9, 1956, all of England watched on TV as he laid his 17-year-old assistant on a table, turned on a huge, madly spinning buzz saw, and appeared to cut her in half, right across the stomach. Then he pretended to try to wake up the girl, but she didn't move. She just lay on the table, still and pale. This was part of the act—to give everyone a last heart-pounding moment before inviting her to get up and take her bows, all in one piece. But the program had run overtime, and at that moment the announcer came on to say goodnight and the TV show was over.

The switchboard at the studio was jammed as thousands of horrified Brits phoned in to protest the gory television murder. The next day, newspaper headlines everywhere reassured people: "THE GIRL SAWN IN HALF IS ALL RIGHT." Sorcar, who always worked hard for his publicity, had accidentally gotten a whole lot of it.

Protul Chandra Sorcar is remembered as more than a great magician. As well as traveling and performing throughout the world, he wrote 22 books on the history and practice of magic, and won many awards, including the prestigious *Padmashri* (Lotus) award from the government of India. As a successful and dedicated performer, Sorcar became an unofficial ambassador of magic and of India. But he didn't do it for the glory. He did it for the love of magic. As he put it: "When asleep I breathe magic. When awake I make magic."

# X-RAY EYES

Wow your audience, as P.C. Sorcar wowed people all over the world, with your X-ray eyes that can see right through cards.

**MATERIALS:**
Deck of playing cards.

Have a volunteer shuffle the cards and hand the deck back to you. Spread the cards out on the table, face down. Choose three cards out of the 52 and identify them without looking at them.

## HOW IT'S DONE

After the volunteer hands the deck back to you, talk a bit about the amazing X-ray eyes you were born with as you tip the deck for a moment, just far enough that you can take a peek at the bottom card. Memorize it. Spread the cards out face down, remembering where the bottom card is (say it's the queen of spades).

Point to some other card and identify it as the queen of spades. Then pick it up, not letting anyone else see it. Nod in satisfaction as though you were right, memorize it (say it's the five of hearts), and keep it in your hand. Now point to another card—not the bottom card—and identify it as the five of hearts. Pick it up, hiding it from view,

and nod again. Keep that card (say it's the nine of clubs) in your hand with the other one.

Then point to the bottom card and identify it as the nine of clubs. Pick it up, put it with the others, and remind the audience that you've named the queen of spades, five of hearts, and nine of clubs. Show the cards. Bingo!

# HARRY BLACKSTONE

## UP CLOSE AND PERSONAL
## 1885–1965

**H**ARRY BLACKSTONE became a great magician doing small magic: tricks done by hand, very close to the people watching, with ordinary objects like cards and coins. Skillful, exuberant, and just a bit mischievous, he was adored by thousands of people because he made everyone feel that he was making magic just for them.

Blackstone was born and raised in Chicago. He was a skinny guy with a big head, a trim mustache, lots of white hair like a giant halo, and tons of energy. He had fun doing magic. When Blackstone stepped out on the stage, took off his white gloves, threw them in the air, and turned them into doves, he was chatting and telling jokes the whole time. When he brought out a world map, punched a hole in Turkey, and whipped out a real live turkey, he made awful puns and laughed uproariously. He was so delighted by the magic that you just had to join in the fun—even when he stole your watch, wallet, and keys without you noticing.

Even when things went wrong, Blackstone found a way to enjoy it. One night when the stagehands were late in bringing out a prop, Blackstone announced that he would make all of his assistants vanish instead. He guided them into a tent, whispering instructions, then fired a pistol in the air, and poof!—they were gone.

Blackstone was so crazy about his work that he made magic everywhere—at home, on the train, in a taxi, on the street—with coins, cigars, whatever was handy. In a restaurant he would throw someone's glass in the air and it would vanish. In a coffee shop he once ordered a plain doughnut, then switched it for a chocolate one and complained that the waitress had got it wrong. (He soon confessed and gave her free tickets to his show.)

Blackstone also worked hard to promote his show. The minute he and his crew arrived in a town or city to give a performance, he was out doing appearances at newspaper offices, public events, and hospitals.

Blackstone performed in more towns and traveled farther than any other magician working at the time. He also made more money than any other magician, yet he was always broke. He always insisted on paying the bill at a bar or restaurant, he invited anyone with a hard luck story—especially wannabe magicians—to stay at his home, and he worked 12 or 16 hours every day but encouraged all his young workers to sleep in. Freeloaders took advantage of Blackstone's generosity, and sometimes he got cheated in business.

Fortunately Blackstone always had lots of gigs lined up. People came in droves to see him produce hundreds of flowers from nowhere, pull a burro out of a pile of silk scarves, or transform a feather duster into a live duck. But no matter what illusions Blackstone included in the show, the small magic—the simple tricks that he did by hand—were always the most bewitching. His audiences particularly loved two acts: the "Floating Light Bulb" and the "Dancing Handkerchief."

For the Dancing Handkerchief, Blackstone called to the audience, "May I borrow a gentleman's handkerchief?" Then, eyes twinkling, "A *clean* one, please!" He tied a knot in a corner of the hanky for a "head" and it came to life and escaped, swooping and darting about the stage. When the theater orchestra struck up a bouncy tune, the handkerchief danced along the floor, bobbing and swaying to the beat. Finally the hanky leapt back into Blackstone's hand, where it continued to dance until Blackstone returned it to its owner. At that moment the hanky went still—an ordinary handkerchief once more.

For the Floating Light Bulb, the stage was almost dark. A woman in a gown glided onstage holding a lighted lamp with a long cord that ran backstage. Blackstone unscrewed the bulb, which magically stayed lit. He held it out, then let it go, and there it floated. Blackstone passed a hoop all around the light bulb, showing that no strings were attached. He then walked into the audience. The light bulb followed him and flitted about over everyone's heads. Then Blackstone returned to the stage, caught the bulb, and put it back in the lamp, finishing up one of the most enchanting small tricks in the world of magic.

Blackstone was one of the best-known magicians in the world until the 1950s. Then everything changed. Television was invented, and people stayed home for fun more often instead of going out to see live shows at theaters. Blackstone did a few performances on TV, but he was getting older, and his specialty—small magic, up close and personal—worked best on a real stage. It was time to retire.

Blackstone moved to Hollywood and began to hang out at Bert Wheeler's Hollywood Magic Shop. There he became known to local kids as the old guy with wild white hair who showed them how to do really cool magic tricks. Even at the end of his life, during his last stay in hospital, Blackstone sat up in bed and did small tricks with coins, cards, and dishes for his doctors, nurses, and fellow patients. He was the Great Blackstone to the very end.

# MONEY BUNS

**MATERIALS:**
Bun or roll; dime.

When Harry Blackstone dined with friends, he astonished everyone by doing "small magic" at the table—tricks with spoons, salt shakers, glasses, whatever was there. You can baffle your family by finding cash in a bun.

Open a roll during a meal and find a dime inside.

## HOW IT'S DONE

When the meal includes buns or rolls, hide a dime in your right hand when you sit down to eat. Pick up a bun, push the nail of one finger into the bottom of it to make a slit, and slide in the dime. Start to eat the bun, then stop, stare at it, and shake it next to your ear, saying, "What's in there?" Then break open the bun with both hands, tipping it as you do, to keep the dime-slit out of sight. Stare into the bun with amazement and display it, holding it open, to show everyone the coin you have found inside.

# DOUG HENNING
## MAGICIAN FOR A NEW AGE
## 1947–2000

WHEN TELEVISION BECAME POPULAR in North America in the 1950s, fewer people went out to live theater performances—including magic shows. Then, 20 years later, along came Doug Henning. He put on a big, fun stage magic show and performed on TV, and presto! The excitement of magic was back.

Henning was a young, skinny, sweet guy with a big smile. He didn't look a bit like a magician—no sumptuous costumes, no tuxedo and top hat, no posters advertising him as Henning the Great. He bounced onstage in a shaggy haircut, wearing a tie-dyed T-shirt, blue jeans, and running shoes, and he did incredible tricks.

Henning grew up in Winnipeg, Canada. He fell in love with magic when he was seven years old and spent all his spare time

learning sleight of hand. His plan was to become a doctor so that he could afford his hobby of magic. At medical school he studied the science of illusions—how our eyes and brains work together to see our world, and how the natural gaps and tricks of our senses can be used to make us believe we are seeing the impossible. What makes us believe that a handkerchief can turn into a dove, or a woman sawn in half can be put back together, when we know it can't be done? The more Henning learned, the more excited he was about the art of illusion.

He traveled around the world for a year after he finished school, learning from other magicians, becoming more and more convinced that live stage magic could be revived. When he got home, he begged and borrowed enough money to produce a show called *Spellbound,* which had old tricks, new tricks, and rock music. It opened at a theater in Toronto in 1973 and was a runaway success. A year later Henning took the show to New York, where it was a hit for more than four years. Magic was back, big time.

Henning performed many classic magic tricks, but he always added a playful little twist. In the "Mismade Girl," his version of sawing someone in half, he popped a woman into a tall, narrow, brightly colored box and closed the box by shutting four small cupboard doors in front, one above the other. Then he pushed metal blades through the side of the box, as though slicing the box (and the woman) into four sections. He and his assistants snatched up the sections and danced merrily around the stage with them. Finally they piled them up again, but not in the same order. Henning opened the doors to reveal the woman, who was alive and well, but her "cut-up" sections were all mixed up. She hollered at Henning until he ran over and rearranged the four sections. Out stepped the woman, magically restored.

Then an American network offered to produce a magic extravaganza for TV, and in 1975 *World of Magic* went on the air. Henning insisted that the show be broadcast live, so that viewers could be sure the show wasn't rigged. He wouldn't even allow commercials. Everything had to be done in full view, out in the open.

He got things going with a close up shot of his left hand with a nickel in it. He closed his hand, turned it over, then turned it back, and the nickel was gone. The camera view widened to show both hands, and Henning opened his right hand to reveal that the nickel had magically migrated there.

From there, with his audience of 50 million people totally hooked, Henning went on to pull a few fluttering doves out of the air. He popped them into a cage, borrowed a scarf from someone in the audience and brought a parrot out of the scarf. Then he laid the scarf over the cage and made the whole works disappear. Henning hypnotized his assistant, then floated her in midair, lying down, supported only by her elbow on the microphone stand. Just as the audience started to look for the invisible wires or poles, Henning passed a flaming hoop around her body from head to toe.

Henning wrapped up the show with a new version of Harry Houdini's thrilling "Water Torture Cell" illusion. His assistants handcuffed him and lowered him head first into a glass-fronted tank of water, and a curtain was drawn around the tank. Both tank and curtain sat on a raised platform on legs, so everyone could see there was no trapdoor. A stopwatch on the TV screen ticked the seconds away as viewers got more and more nervous. Sixty seconds, ninety seconds. Had something gone wrong? At two minutes, a hooded assistant rushed offstage to grab an ax, ready to smash the tank open. Half a minute later the assistant pulled the curtain open to reveal an empty tank. Then the assistant tore off his hood—and it was Henning!

The show was a fantastic success. People of all ages were enchanted by Henning's cheery personality, his bright, quick style, and his superb skill at magic.

Henning made magic popular again and he opened doors for other magicians to work onstage and in movies and television. As he had known all along, everyone loves magic, and magic does not go out of style. It just needs a new look from time to time.

# ANTI-GRAVITY WATER

**Doug Henning appeared to defy gravity by levitating people. You can levitate a small amount of water in a rolled-up $5.00 bill.**

**MATERIALS:** Thumb tip (a simple plastic gizmo that fits on the end of your thumb, available in magic shops); piece of paper 3 inches (7.5 cm) square, small glass of water.

Borrow a $5.00 bill from a volunteer and roll it into a tube. Hold the tube vertically. Crumple the paper into a wad and stuff it in the bottom end, explaining that it will act as a cork. Pour water into the top of the tube, then pull out the ball of paper. The water stays magically suspended in the tube. After the oohs and aahs have died down, put the "cork" back in, pour out the water, and return the bill to the volunteer for inspection.

## HOW IT'S DONE

Before you perform, cover your thumb with the thumb tip (1). Roll the bill around that thumb to make your tube (2), and leave the tip in the tube when you take out your thumb as shown. Turn the tube over before inserting the paper wad so that you are pouring the water into the thumb tip (3). At the end of the trick, after pouring out the water, reinsert your thumb into the thumb tip and pull it out as you unroll the bill.

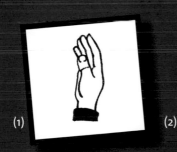  

(1)  (2)  (3)

# SIEGFRIED & ROY

## WILD MAGIC MAKERS
## 1939– & 1944–

**S**IEGFRIED FISCHBACHER AND ROY HORN brought magic to new heights of glamour and excitement. For more than 13 years, their unique blend of manmade magic (high-tech special effects) and natural magic (rare exotic animals) was the most popular show in Las Vegas, Nevada, the glitz capital of the world.

Siegfried and Roy didn't know each other when they were growing up in Germany after World War II, but both were already embarked on their life work. Siegfried was eight when he got hold of a book on magic tricks and learned them all. Meanwhile, Roy spent his days with his pet and soulmate, Hexe (pronounced "Heck-seh"), half-dog and half-wolf. He also made friends with Chico, a cheetah at the local zoo, and eventually he was permitted to feed and groom Chico.

Siegfried and Roy were teenagers when they went to work aboard a German cruise ship. Siegfried put on magic shows in between shifts as a bartender, and Roy, a bellboy, began to assist him as he made coins vanish, conjured live birds out of red silk scarves, and made canes float through the air. One evening Roy asked Siegfried whether he could make a cheetah disappear. Siegfried said, "In magic, anything is possible." The next time the ship sailed, Roy smuggled Chico aboard.

Three days later they presented their new act. Siegfried tore up a small stuffed leopard and tossed the parts into a box. Then he closed the box, the ship's orchestra played a suspenseful tune, the box was opened—and Chico sprang out and wowed the audience. Every magician needs a signature act, and Siegfried and Roy now had theirs: Siegfried's mastery at sleight of hand, spiced up with Roy's way with animals—especially wild ones.

In 1967 Siegfried and Roy took their magic act to Las Vegas. They performed in variety shows with their doves and rabbits, and with Chico and a new cheetah named Simba. The act was a hit, even though Vegas was known as a town where no one went to magic shows. As their performance got bigger, they acquired their first Siberian tiger, Sahra, and a ferocious-looking 650-pound (290-

kilogram) lion named Leo. A leopard and a panther came next. For Sahra they built a grand finale illusion. Siegfried made her vanish, then brought her back atop an enormous glowing mirror ball at center stage. The ball rose, revolved, and appeared to float high above the audience with Sahra aboard.

Siegfried and Roy's wild animals shared their life offstage as well, on a large estate called the Jungle Palace, home to swans, dogs, flamingoes, flocks of nightingales, and more than 60 big cats. For years, Roy swam laps with the cats in the morning and slept with a lion or tiger every night. Before each show, he meditated with one of the starring animals.

In 1987 a new hotel, the Mirage, invited Siegfried and Roy to put on their own big show, in a new theater built especially for them. They spent two years planning and designing the show. And what a show! The theater had 1,500 seats, 75 tons (68 tonnes) of scenery, and a set of lights so complicated that seven computer boards were needed to run it. Michael Jackson wrote and recorded special music for it, 30 big cats took turns starring onstage, and the cast and crew of humans numbered 160.

The show opened with an upbeat, sparkly laser and

dance number. Siegfried and Roy stepped out of smoke-filled glass containers and made a motorcycle, an elephant, and each other vanish. They floated through rings in the air. They acted out fairy tales in which brave heroes battled wicked queens and a flame-spitting dragon three stories high. Then came the animals—dazzling under the lights. Lions turned into panthers and panthers into lions. Siegfried levitated a tiger over the heads of the audience, the cats appeared to fly across the stage, and Roy rode a white tiger into a night sky. Tigers became women, then became tigers again—all amid maximum glitz and glam with lasers, holograms, and crashing music by a full orchestra.

The performance on the evening of October 3, 2003, was like any other show. Everything was going great until Roy walked onstage with Montecore, a seven-year-old tiger who had performed in several shows. Instead of lying down when he was supposed to, Montecore growled, then pounced, sank his teeth into Roy's neck, and dragged him offstage. Roy was rushed to the hospital with terrible injuries. "Don't shoot the tiger," he managed to say before he lost consciousness.

Roy survived the attack, but the show did not. After more than 12 years and 5,600 sold-out performances, Siegfried and Roy's one-of-a-kind show at the Mirage was cancelled. No one knows whether it will ever be produced again, or whether any other conjuror can bring the natural magic of tigers and lions to the big stage. But Siegfried and Roy showed the world that a grand, spectacular magic act could not only survive onstage in an entertainment center like Las Vegas, it could thrive.

# MONEY SWITCH

**Show off your Siegfried-and-Roy-style sleight of hand by turning money into paper.**

**MATERIALS:** Handkerchief or light cloth napkin; elastic band; piece of newspaper the size of a $5.00 bill.

Borrow a $5.00 bill from a friend. Crumple it into a ball and hold the ball between your right thumb and index finger. Have your friend drape the handkerchief over your hand and take the crumpled bill from you—still covered by the handkerchief—and hang on to it. Meanwhile, reach into your pocket with your right hand and pull out an elastic band. Put the elastic around the bill, nice and tight. Say some magic words, then have your friend take off the elastic. The money has disappeared, leaving a wad of newspaper in its place!

## HOW IT'S DONE

Before the show, crumple the piece of newspaper and hide it in your right hand under the three fingers you aren't using. When you are before your audience, as your friend puts the handkerchief over the bill, switch it with the crumpled newspaper and hide the bill in your fingers. When you reach into your pocket to take out the elastic, drop the bill in your pocket.

**D**AVID COPPERFIELD is a state-of-the-art conjuror. He combines classic illusions with high-tech tools—lasers, pyrotechnics, satellites, TV, and the Internet—to make a brand-new kind of magic.

When Copperfield was growing up in New Jersey in the 1960s, he saw a magician perform on TV, and he knew right away that he wanted to be one, too. At age 10 he was performing at parties as Davino the Boy Magician, at age 16 he was teaching magic at a university, and at age 18 he had his own stage show. He was so good at levitation that one reporter wrote, "He can float anything from a dancing cane to a hypnotized lady in midair."

That was in 1975. Twenty-five years later, Copperfield's show opened with an empty glass elevator that descended to the stage. Some spooky fog rolled in around it, rock music pulsed through the

theater, and with a great flash of light the elevator doors opened and out stepped Copperfield. He turned a bit of tissue paper into a paper rose, then set it on fire and transformed it into a real rose. He sawed himself in half with a laser instead of a buzz saw, then pulled himself together. Next he levitated himself, with a special-effects twist—he appeared to fly into a giant fan and get blown out over the audience. Back onstage, he asked two young women in the audience to come up and help him. One second, two seconds, and they found that they were wearing each other's underwear.

In one of his most baffling and hilarious tricks, Copperfield would throw 13 beach balls every which way into the audience. The people who caught them went up on stage, and pow! With a flash and a puff of smoke, the 13 people were gone. Copperfield pointed to the back of the theater and there they were, just as surprised as everyone else.

Copperfield has done other illusions that were just too big for a stage. He once made a seven-ton (6.3-tonne) jet plane disappear. He has levitated a Ferrari, walked through (not on) the Great Wall of China, floated across the Grand Canyon, and made the Statue of Liberty vanish in front of a live audience seated on outdoor bleachers in New York City.

How does he do it? His methods are a deep secret, and to make sure no one figures them out, he works up several ways to do each illusion. That means hours and hours of practice every week. In one spectacular stunt, Copperfield escaped from a straitjacket while hanging upside down from a burning rope, over flaming metal spikes. He worked on that trick every day for a year. Each day he added more fire and hung a bit higher in the air. He videotaped every practice session and studied the tapes to figure out what he needed to fix. Copperfield's trick of flying through the air without any wires took even longer to learn—seven years.

Over time, Copperfield has taken advantage of new technology to add special effects to his show. He used satellites in developing an amazing trick in which audience members appeared to be transported halfway across the world in an instant. A screen onstage showed a live satellite video feed from a sunny beach in Thailand, where some friends of Copperfield's were relaxing. They chatted together via video linkup. He then asked a volunteer from the audience to come onstage and write out a huge postcard, and he took a Polaroid of the volunteer holding the card. Then poof! They both disappeared from the theater and appeared

on the video from the beach in Thailand, holding up the Polaroid of the postcard. In the blink of an eye the two were back onstage, and Copperfield took off his shoes and poured out sand. Cameras don't lie, right?

The new challenges Copperfield has set for himself include straightening the Leaning Tower of Pisa, making the moon vanish, and working with Internet technology to create the world's first online magic. To make his visions come true, Copperfield may have to be in many places at once. Can he do that for real? "Practice, practice, practice," he says, "and never consider anything impossible."

# WATER TRANSPLANT

No one but David Copperfield knows how he can transport 13 volunteers from the stage to the back of a theater in the blink of an eye. And no one will guess how you get a cup of water to move from a paper bag to a bowl without anyone noticing.

**MATERIALS:** Plastic or metal bowl large and deep enough to fit a small paper cup full of water; paper bag (lunch bag size); three small paper cups (all the same color and design); water.

(1)

(2)

(3)

(4)

Fill a cup with water and put it in the bowl. Move the cup of water into a paper bag, then crumple up the bag—with no sign of spilled water.

## HOW IT'S DONE

Before the show, carefully snip the top rim and the bottom off of one of the paper cups. Tuck this "shell" into one of the other cups (1). Pour some water into the cup without the shell.

When you are before your audience, have the bag, the bowl, and the two cups sitting on the table. Show them that one cup is full of water. Say that you are going to pour the water into the other cup, and do so (2). Place the cup (with shell and water) into the bowl. Then say that you want to put the cup of water in the bag. Reach into the bowl and pull out only the shell, holding it

so it looks like a cup full of water (3) and so no one can see the bottom is missing. Gently put the shell in the bag (4) and lift the bag as though trying not to spill the water.

Now, moving fast, crumple up the bag and toss it over your shoulder. "Hey, where did the water go?" Look around for it, and act surprised when you find it in the bowl.

# Sources

## Books

Abram, David. *Spell of the Sensuous: Perception and Language in a More-Than-Human World*. New York: Pantheon, 1996.

Becker, Herbert L. *All the Secrets of Magic Revealed*. Hollywood, FL: Lifetime Books, 1994.

Blackstone, Harry. *Blackstone's Tricks Anyone Can Do*. Secaucus, NJ: Carol Publishing Group, 1983.

Blackstone, Harry Jr., with Charles and Regina Reynolds. *The Blackstone Book of Magic and Illusion*. New York: Newmarket Press, 1985.

Brandon, Ruth. *The Life and Many Deaths of Harry Houdini*. London: Secker & Warburg, 1993.

Cannell, J.C. *The Secrets of Houdini*. New York: Dover Publications, 1973.

Christopher, Milbourne. *Houdini: A Pictorial Life*. New York: Crowell, 1976.

———. *Houdini: The Untold Story*. New York: Crowell, 1969.

———. *Illustrated History of Magic*. New York: Crowell, 1973.

———. *Milbourne Christopher's Magic Book*. New York: Crowell, 1977.

Clark, Hyla M. *The World's Greatest Magic*. New York: Crown, 1976.

Coleman, Earle Jerome. *Magic: A Reference Guide*. New York: Greenwood Press, 1987.

Dawes, Edwin A. *The Great Illusionists*. Newton Abbot, UK: David & Charles, 1979.

——— and Arthur Setterington. *The Encyclopedia of Magic*. New York: Gallery Books, 1986.

Eldin, Peter. *Magic*. New York: Kingfisher, 1997.

Ernst, John. *Escape King: The Story of Harry Houdini*. Englewood Cliffs, NJ: Prentice-Hall, 1975.

Fischbacher, Siegfried, and Roy Horn. *Siegfried and Roy: Mastering the Impossible*. New York: Morrow, 1992.

Gibson, Walter B. *The Complete Beginner's Guide to Magic*. Hollywood, FL: Lifetime Books, 1996.

———. *Mastering Magic: Secrets of the Great Magicians Revealed*. New York: F. Fell, 1977.

———. *The Master Magicians*. Secaucus, NJ: Citadel Press, 1966.

Henning, Doug. *Houdini: His Legend and His Magic*. New York: Times Books, 1977.

Jay, Ricky. *Jay's Journal of Anomalies: Conjurors, Cheats, Hustlers, Hoaxsters...* New York: Farrar, Straus, Giroux, 2001.

Lewis, Shari, and Abraham B. Hurwitz. *Magic for Non-Magicians*. Los Angeles: J.P. Tarcher, 1975.

Parrish, Robert. *Great Tricks Revisited: Thoughts on Classics*. Glenwood, IL: D. Meyer Magic Books, 1995.

Randi, James. *Conjuring*. New York: St. Martin's Press, 1992.

———. *Houdini: His Life and Art*. New York: Grosset & Dunlap, 1976.

———. *The Magic World of the Amazing Randi*. Holbrook, MA: Bob Adams Inc., 1989.

Robert-Houdin, Jean Eugene. *Memoirs of Jean Eugene Robert-Houdin*. Trans. Lascelles Wraxall. New York: Dover Publications, 1964.

Schiffman, Nathaniel. *Abracadabra! Secret Methods Magicians and Others Use to Deceive Their Audience*. Amherst, NY: Prometheus Books, 1997.

Severn, Bill. *Bill Severn's Big Book of Magic*. New York: D. McKay, 1973.

———. *Bill Severn's Guide to Magic as a Hobby*. New York: D. McKay, 1979.

Singer, Mark. "Secrets of the Magus," in *Life Stories: Profiles from the New Yorker*, ed. David Remnick. New York: Random House, 2000.

Sorcar, P.C. *P.C. Sorcar on Magic: Reminiscences and Selected Tricks*. Calcutta: Indrajal Publications, 1960.

———. *Indian Magic*. Delhi: Hind Pocket Books, 1970.

Steinmeyer, Jim. *How Magicians Invented the Impossible and Learned to Disappear*. New York: Carroll & Graf, 2003.

Tarr, Bill. *101 Easy-to-Learn Classic Magic Tricks*. New York: Random House, 1977.

Thaw, Barbara L., and Stephen J. Ronson. *The Armchair Magicians*. New York: Bantam Doubleday Dell, 1994.

Waldron, Daniel. *Blackstone: A Magician's Life*. Glenwood, IL: D. Meyer Magic Books, 1999.

Waters, T.A. *The Encyclopedia of Magic and Magicians*. New York: Facts on File, 1988.

# Video

Grand Illusions: The Story of Magic. 6 vols. (1: Father of Modern Magic; 2: Harry Houdini; 3: Herrmanns; 4: Greats of Modern Magic; 5: Weird Magic; 6: Death by Magic). Writer: Chris Deacon. Producer: Paragon Productions. 2002.

# Web

Crasson, Sara. "Magic History and Magical Myths: The Historian's Challenge." www.uelectric.com/pastimes/crasson.htm

London, Scott. "The Ecology of Magic: An Interview with David Abram." *Insight & Outlook* (radio series), 1999: http://www.scottlondon.com/insight/scripts/abram.html

PageWise, Inc. "Doug Henning: Biography." http://nvnv.essortment.com/doughenningbio_rxez.htm

Sorcar, P.C. www.pcsorcarmagician.com.

Steele, Margaret. "Adelaide, Queen of Magic." www.amazingmagicshow.com/Addie.htm

H.W. Wilson Co., "David Copperfield." *Biographies Plus Illustrated.* http://vnweb.hwwilsonweb.com/hww/shared/shared_main.jhtml;jsessionid=T5X0S01HB2WoLQA3DILSFGGADUNGIIVo?_requestid=93134

H.W. Wilson Co., "Doug Henning." *Biographies Plus Illustrated.* http://vnweb.hwwilsonweb.com/hww/shared/shared_main.jhtml;jsessionid=T5X0S01HB2WoLQA3DILSFGGADUNGIIVo?_requestid=93134

H.W. Wilson Co., "Siegfried & Roy." *Biographies Plus Illustrated.* http://vnweb.hwwilsonweb.com/hww/shared/shared_main.jhtml;jsessionid=T5X0S01HB2WoLQA3DILSFGGADUNGIIVo?_requestid=93134

# Interview

Manick Sorcar, May 27, 2004.

# Periodicals

Bertram, Stan. "The Magic of Those Days." *Genii* (January 1975).

Christy, George. "Where the Wild Things Are." *Interview* (August 1993), p. 54.

Deachman, Bruce. "The Enduring Magic of Magic." *Ottawa Citizen* (November 4, 2000), p. N1.

Fink, Jerry. "Siegfried and Roy Still Making Magic at Mirage." *Las Vegas Sun* (July 18, 2003).

Gliatto, Tom, et al. "Savage Betrayal." *People* (October 20, 2003), pp. 70–74, 76.

Gubernick, Lisa, and Peter Newcomb. "Now You See It, Now You Don't." *Forbes* (September 27, 1993), pp. 88–92.

Herrington, Richard. "Levitation and Levity." *Washington Post* (June 9, 1984), p. D7.

Hutchings, David. "Menagerie a Deux." *People* (January 11, 1993), pp. 98–102.

"Jean Eugene Robert-Houdin" (obituary). *New York Times* (July 4, 1871).

Jillette, P. "The Dark Arts." *Rolling Stone* 935 (November 13, 2003), p. 53.

Kernan, Michael. "David Copperfield's Monumental Magic Act." *Washington Post* (September 27, 1982), p. C1.

Larsen, Bill. "Doug Henning's World of Magic." *Genii* (February 1976), pp. 98–102.

McKinley, Jesse. "Doug Henning, a Superstar of Illusion, Is Dead at 52." *New York Times* (February 9, 2000), p. B10.

Polanski, Roman. "The Most Popular Illusionist in the World." *Interview* (January 1996), pp. 94–97.

Riches, Hester. "Copperfield's Art is Enhancing Reality." *Vancouver Sun* (December 8, 1994), p. C3.

"Roar Power." *Guardian TV* (April 17, 2003), pp. 9–10.

"Under Her Skirts: How Mme. Herrmann Imported Rare Silk Patterns." *Los Angeles Times* (December 6, 1897), p. 3.

Wilson, Elizabeth. "On Doug Henning and Modern Magic." *Genii* (February 1976), pp. 95–96.

Witchel, Alex. "A Maestro of the Magic Arts Returns to His Roots." *New York Times* (November 24, 1996), pp. H4/11.

Zehme, Bill. "Shazam!" *Esquire* (April 1994), pp. 90–95.

———. "What I've Learned: Siegfried and Roy." *Esquire* 134:2 (August 2000), pp. 108–9.

# Index

Page references to photos are in *italics*.

# Acknowledgments

My thanks to Karen Schendlinger and Donimo for research; Jill Mandrake and Manick Sorcar for information and support; the Letterheads (Sarah Leavitt, Billeh Nickerson, Ian Reid, Alexandra Samuel, Rhonda Waterfall) for reads and critiques; Pam Robertson and Elizabeth McLean for editing; Warren Clark and Irvin Cheung for tricky visuals; Karin Ades, Nora D. Randall, Jo Cook, Saeko Usukawa, Sarah Leavitt, Barbara Zatyko, Gordon MacLachlan, and Joe McDermott for sustenance; Karen Schendlinger, Minna Schendlinger, and Julia Perroni for love; and Stephen Osborne for magic.

# Photo Credits

# About the Author

Mary Schendlinger grew up in Waukesha, Wisconsin, in a house full of books. When not reading, she was busy writing and drawing her own stories, a pursuit encouraged by her aunt Betty, who gave Mary her first typewriter. Mary has been typing ever since.

Today, Mary is an experienced writer and editor of books, magazines, Web sites, and even comics, which she illustrates herself. She teaches courses for writers and editors at Simon Fraser University and at writers' conferences. Mary has lived in Vancouver, BC for 35 years.